TEENY-TINY
and the Witch-Woman

by Barbara K. Walker

Illustrated by Michael Foreman

Andersen Press London / Hutchinson of Australia

Text ©1975 by Barbara K. Walker. Illustrations ©1975 by Michael Foreman. First published in Great Britain in 1977 by Andersen Press Ltd., 62-65 Chandos Place, London WC2. Reprinted 1986. Published in Australia by Hutchinson Publishing Group (Australia) Pty. Ltd., Melbourne, Victoria 3122. All rights reserved. Published in the United States by Pantheon Books, a division of Random House, Inc. Printed in Italy by Grafiche AZ, Verona. ISBN 0 905478 09 6

Once there was and twice there wasn't, long ago, a family with three brothers — Big-One, In-the-Middle, and Teeny-Tiny. Every day their mother said, "You can play anywhere in the village, but do not go into the forest to play. Your granny says a witch-woman lives there, where the trees are darkest. She eats little children, and uses their bones to make the fence around her house."

Big-One and In-the-Middle laughed, but Teeny-Tiny shivered. He was glad to play there in the warm sunshine, away from the forest.

One morning, though, when no one was looking, Big-One said, "Let's go into the forest to play."

"Yes," agreed In-the-Middle. "I'm not afraid of any old witch-woman! Come on, Teeny-Tiny."

Now, Teeny-Tiny didn't want to go, but he went anyway. "I'll keep my eyes open and my legs ready to run," he told himself.

Big-One, In-the-Middle, and Teeny-Tiny played all day in the forest. The deep, dark shadows made fine hiding places, and the wild berries in the clearings made a delicious lunch.

Little by little, the shadows grew longer. The boys looked for the path to the village, but no matter where they looked they could find no path at all. At last Teeny-Tiny climbed a tree to look farther. "I see a light," he called. "Let's go there. It may be a house."

They walked and they walked till they came to a little house, all by itself in the darkest part of the forest. All around the house there was a knobby white fence. The gate clattered as they pushed at it.

Just then, the door of the house opened, C-R-E-A-K, and an old woman stood in the doorway. But what a strange old woman she was, with her nose turned down and her chin turned up, and just the points of her teeth showing.

"Come in. Come in, my children!" she called. And she beckoned with her bony finger.

Big-One and In-the-Middle started toward the open door, but Teeny-Tiny whispered, "Wait! Remember what our granny said."

"Oh, that can't be the witch-woman," said Big-One. "She's so kind to ask us in."

"I'm tired," said In-the-Middle. "You're just *afraid* because you're *little*."

"Afraid?" The old woman cackled. She had heard them! "You needn't be afraid of *me*. I *love* little children. Come in," she coaxed. "Stay with me and share my dinner. Your own nice, warm beds are far away, but I have room for all of you in my little house tonight. Tomorrow I shall show you your way home. But come now, and smell the good dinner I have ready for you."

And the old woman hobbled over to the fireplace. She took off the lid of her huge iron kettle, and, *Mmmmn,* what good smells came out of that kettle!

"Come on," said Big-One. "I'm going inside."

"Good boy," said the old woman. "You may call me Auntie." And she waited by the door as In-the-Middle and Teeny-Tiny followed Big-One into the house.

While the old woman set three extra places at the dinner table, Teeny-Tiny looked around at all that he could see. Over in the corner of the room was a crooked little wooden cage. "Auntie," he asked, "what do you keep in your cage?"

"In my *cage?* Oh, sometimes I keep stray dogs and sometimes I keep stray cats," answered the old woman.

"And sometimes stray *children?*" wondered Teeny-Tiny. But he didn't say anything.

It was a very good dinner that the old woman scooped up out of the kettle, with bits of tender meat and plenty of rice. The boys ate and ate, and the good food and the warm fire made them very sleepy.

"You must be tired," said the old woman. "Come now, into the bedroom and I'll put you into my nice, soft beds." Sure enough, she tucked Big-One into one bed, In-the-Middle into a second bed, and Teeny-Tiny into a third bed. "Now, sleep well," she said, "and tomorrow, just *see* if I don't show you your way home!" Leaving the door ajar, she went out into the kitchen.

Teeny-Tiny waited until he heard her picking up the dishes, and then he tiptoed to the window to look outside. The moon had risen, and the moonlight shone down on that knobby white fence. Was it a *wooden* fence? No. It was made of *bones*

—leg bones and arm bones, little *people* bones. Teeny-Tiny stared at the fence, and then he looked at Big-One and at In-the-Middle, already sound asleep. They didn't know, but Teeny-Tiny did.

This was indeed the house of the witch-woman their granny had told them about!

Teeny-Tiny tiptoed back to bed. As he lay there, he could see the old woman tying pieces of rope together. He could hear her sharpening and sharpening a great, long knife. And all the while she hummed a sleep-sleep-sleepy song.

After a while, the old woman called, "Who is awake and who is asleep?"

Now the others were asleep, but Teeny-Tiny was not.

"The littlest one is awake," he answered.

"What! Teeny-Tiny, why don't you sleep?" asked the old woman.

"Well, Auntie, my mother always cooks me an egg before I go to bed. *Then* I go to sleep," said Teeny-Tiny.

So the old woman cooked an egg, and Teeny-Tiny ate it. But still he did not go to sleep.

After a while she called again, "Who is awake and who is asleep?"

"The littlest one is awake," answered Teeny-Tiny.

"What? Still awake? What will help you go to sleep?" the old woman asked.

"Well, Auntie, my mother gives me popcorn and raisins to eat at bedtime. *Then* I go to sleep," said Teeny-Tiny.

So the old woman brought him popcorn and raisins. But still he did not go to sleep.

After a while she called again, "Who is awake, and who is asleep?"

"The littlest one is awake," answered Teeny-Tiny.

"What! Still awake, are you? What can I get you that will help you to sleep?" she asked.

"Well, Auntie, all that popcorn has made me thirsty. At home, when I am thirsty, my mother goes to the well to fetch me water in a sieve. When she brings it back, I drink it. *Then* I go to sleep," said Teeny-Tiny.

As the old woman bent over to fetch her sieve, a cake of soap fell out of her apron pocket. "Oh dear," the old woman mumbled aloud. "My magic objects. Better to leave them here safe than lose them outside in the dark by the well." She picked up the cake of soap. Then, reaching into her apron pocket, she took out what was left—a needle and a short, sharp knife—and she laid all three things on a high shelf. Then she opened the door softly and started toward the well.

All along, Teeny-Tiny had been listening carefully. As soon as the old woman was gone, he shook his brothers. "Wake up!" he whispered. "Auntie *is* that witch-woman! Her fence is made of people's bones, and she has already sharpened her long knife. If we do not hurry, *we'll* be her dinner tomorrow." Big-One and In-the-Middle heard him, and how they scrambled out of bed!

As they were running through the door, Teeny-Tiny remembered the magic objects the witch-woman had so carefully laid on the high shelf—a cake of soap, a needle, and a short, sharp knife.

"Lift me up," he said to Big-One. "If she *says* they're magic, they just may *be* magic. I'll take them along and see." One, two, three—he tucked them into his pocket, and then ran with his brothers down the moonlit path.

As for the old woman, she couldn't catch any water in the sieve, and she *couldn't* catch any water in the sieve. And because witches are not very bright without their magic, she couldn't understand why. So home she went.

When she looked for Teeny-Tiny he was gone, and so were his brothers. So away she went, running after them.

Now, Teeny-Tiny was watching behind him. As the old woman came closer and closer, he took out the cake of soap. "I'll try this first," he said. "If it *isn't* magic, at least she may slip on it, and then we can get away from her."

And he threw the cake of soap right into her path.

"Oh!" she cried. "You took my magic soap from my little shelf!" And she shook her fist at Teeny-Tiny. Just then, the cake of soap began to *grow* and GROW. It became a mountain, slippery all around. The boys kept on running, glad of that soap.

But the old woman slipped and slithered, trying to get up over the mountain. "It's no use," she said at last. "I'll run around it." And she ran and ran till she came to the other side. "Now I'll catch you!" she cried. And Teeny-Tiny heard her.

They kept running and running, till Teeny-Tiny could hear the witch-woman's apron flapping.

Then carefully, he picked the needle out of his pocket. "Whether it's magic or not, I'll prick her with this sharp needle," he said to himself. But, *whoops!* It slipped out of his hand and fell behind him.

"Oh!" cried the witch-woman. "You found my magic *needle,* too!" And she shook her fist at Teeny-Tiny. At that moment, the needle began to *grow* and GROW, until it became a whole *mountain* of needles, all sticky and pricky and sharp as they could be.

Well, the boys ran on, but the witch-woman had to stop because of the needles. She tried and tried to get over those needles. At last she said, "It's no use. I'll run around them." And she ran and ran till she came to the other side. "*Now* I'll catch you!" she cried.

They kept running and running and running. Teeny-Tiny could hear the old woman panting and puffing just behind them. With all his strength, he threw the knife on the path right in front of the witch-woman. "It's our only chance," he said. "If it *isn't* magic, at least she may cut her foot on it, and then we can get away from her."

"Oh!" she cried. "You took my magic *knife,* too!" And she shook her fist at Teeny-Tiny. At that moment, CRICK-CRACK! That sharp knife cut a crack in the earth so long and so wide that the witch-woman couldn't run around it, and she couldn't jump over it. Shaking both fists, she shouted, "I'll get you the *next* time!" And she turned around and hobbled home.

The three boys never stopped running till they got to their own house. As for that witch-woman, may she wait a long, long time before she hears a knock at her door again.